Get Outside
MAKE FOREST FACES AND MUD MONSTERS

EMILY KINGTON

HUNGRY TOMATO™

CONTENTS

FOREST FACES AND MUD MONSTERS

Going outside is lots of fun, and we can get crafty at the same time. You'll play with shadows, plant some seeds, and make fun projects from things you can find outside.

Get your rain boots on and go on a scavenger hunt. Turn the page to see what things you'll need to find . . .

HELPFUL TOOLS

Gloves
Rain boots
Old bag to carry items home
Small trowel or old spoon
Scissors

You will need a grown-up to help make these fun nature projects.

SCAVENGER HUNT

You need to find...

Moss

Dig it up from the forest floor. It's best if it has a little dirt.

Sticks

Always be on the lookout for sticks of all different sizes.

Leaves

Find dry leaves of all shapes and sizes.

Stones and Pebbles

Look for different shapes, sizes, and colors.

YOU WILL ALSO NEED

Pencil
Pad of paper
Acrylic paint
Martker
String
Plastic container
Trowel
Wooden skewer
Hole punch
White craft glue
Egg carton
Growing soil
Black garbage bag
Spray bottle
Old plant pots
Old milk jug

Seeds and Cones

Pine cones and seeds will look great on your projects.

Mud

The stickier the better. You could also use paper clay.

FIND SOME MONSTERS

See what kinds of faces you can find in the woods!

SCORE YOUR MONSTER FACES!

On a scale of one to five . . .

How scary is it?

How cool is it?

Take a closer look at the trees and fallen branches on the ground.

If you can, take some photos of what you find.

Here is what we found!

Only half a face on this one.
Scary score: 1   **Cool score:** 3

A one-eyed monster!
Monster score: 3   **Cool score:** 3

Definitely a zombie!
Monster score: 3   **Cool score:** 2

Is that a sleeping bear?
Monster score: 2   **Cool score:** 5

This monster is green!
Monster score: 3   **Cool score:** 5

A friendly tree alien!
Monster score: 3   **Cool score:** 4

Just what we're looking for!
Monster score: 5   **Cool score:** 5

SHADOW PLAY

This is one is for walks on sunny days.

Have some fun with shadows on trees.

When the sun is low, you get very, very, tall.

Your shadow will do everything you do!

Have fun with your shadows. If you can, take some pictures. They are fun to frame!

Sometimes you can follow your shadow.

Your shadow can even be by your side.

Make a shadow painting

You don't need to be really good at drawing if you use the sun.

1 Choose something that you want to draw around.

2 Rest the pad against a wall. Make sure the sun is behind you. Draw around the shadows in pencil.

3 Color in your drawing with a marker.

4 Add some seeds and leaves. Add color with some paint.

This is a super easy way to draw!

MUD MONSTERS

Make your own mud monsters!

YOU WILL NEED
Seeds and catkins
Acorn tops
Small sticks
Leaves
Dry grass
Pine cones
Seed pods
Plastic container
Trowel
Water
Wooden skewer
String
Acrylic paint
Paintbrush

1 Dig up some mud and put it into an old container. Add dirt or water until it feels like wet clay.

2 Make the mud into a face. It needs to be thick enough to scoop out a mouth.

Make a nose from extra mud. Use the wooden skewer to make nostrils!

Push leaves into the mud for hair.

3 Roll mud into a ball and shape the head. Paint an acorn top to make the eye.

Push sticks into the mud for legs and seed pods for arms.

Make a fishing pole with a stick and some string.

4 Make this porcupine using a pine cone for the body.

Make a nose out of mud and push it into the top of the cone. Use seeds for eyes.

Tuck dry grass into the cone for the spines.

Make a different monster every time!

WOOD FORT

Watch animals and birds from your secret fort!

YOU WILL NEED

One long, strong stick
Sticks
Moss
Leaves

1 Put one end of the long stick on a low tree branch. Put the other end on the ground.

Lay more sticks on each side of the strong stick.

2 Use moss to fill in gaps between the sticks.

3 Cover with leaves so animals don't spot your fort!

See what kinds of critters you can see!

NOW WE ARE MONSTERS!

Make yourself look wild!

1 Choose a photo of yourself or have one taken.

Seeds

Leaves

Acorn tops

Moss

Seed pods

Dry leaves

Dry flower petals

Flowers

Pine cones

Grass

Small sticks

2 Decorate your photo with things you find outside!

PLANTING SEEDS

Start your own garden!

Seeds
Growing soil
Egg carton
Spray bottle
Black garbage bag
Plastic container

1 Make holes in the bottom of an egg carton. Fill the pods with growing soil and plant the seeds.

2 Fill a plastic container with a little bit of water. Put the egg carton into the water.

Take the carton out when the top of the soil is wet.

Pour the water out of the container.

3 Put the carton back in the container. Cover with part of a garbage bag.

Set in a warm place.

Use a spray bottle to keep the soil watered.

4 When the seeds start growing, move them to a bigger pot.

Care for them inside until it is warm outside!

Take care of your plants!

YOU WILL NEED
String
White craft glue
Old plant pots
Stones
Old milk jug
Wooden skewer

1 Starting at the bottom, wrap the string once around the pot. Glue as you go. You only need to glue the first time around.

Keep wrapping the string around the pot until you get to the top. Glue the top row in place.

2 Have a grown-up help you make holes in the lid of an old milk jug with a wooden skewer.

20

Look at all the
colors!

BARK ART

Make animals out of things you can find outside!

YOU WILL NEED
Bark
Spray bottle
Acrylic paint
Paintbrush

1 Find a piece of bark that looks like an animal. This one looks like an alligator!

2 Find another piece of bark for your animal to rest on.

3 Make sure you are outside for this next part!

Put some paint into the spray bottle and add a tiny bit of water. Shake to mix the paint and water.

Spray away! Add eyes and teeth.

Hide your art in your room or in a garden!

BE CAREFUL OUTSIDE

It's always fun to play outside, but it's a good idea to . . .

. . . take water with you

. . . take a first aid kit for scratches and bug bites

. . . wear clothes and shoes for playing in the woods

. . . tell a grown-up where you are going

Safety First

Don't eat plants, and don't drink water you didn't bring with you.

If you are climbing, make sure you are with a grown-up.

Stay away from wild animals. They could be dangerous!

Be careful near water. It can be deeper than it looks.

Original edition copyright 2019 by Hungry Tomato Ltd.
Copyright © 2020 by Lerner Publishing Group, Inc.

Hungry Tomato® is a trademark of Lerner Publishing Group

Hungry Tomato®
An imprint of Lerner Publishing Group, Inc.
241 First Avenue North
Minneapolis, MN 55401 USA

For reading levels and more information, look up this title at www.lernerbooks.com.

Main body text set in Crossten.

Library of Congress Cataloging-in-Publication Data

Names: Kington, Emily, 1961–– author.
Title: Make forest faces and mud monsters / Emily Kington.
Description: Minneapolis : Hungry Tomato, [2019] | Series: Get outside! | Includes bibliographical references and index.
Identifiers: LCCN 2019016934 (print) | LCCN 2019017725 (ebook) | ISBN 9781541555280 (eb pdf) | ISBN 9781541555273 (lb : alk. paper)
Subjects: LCSH: Nature craft—Juvenile literature. | Outdoor recreation—Juvenile literature.
Classification: LCC TT160 (ebook) | LCC TT160 .K4767 2019 (print) | DDC 745.5—dc23

LC record available at https://lccn.loc.gov/2019016934

Manufactured in the United States of America
1-45931-42825-4/15/2019

PICTURE CREDITS

(abbreviations: t = top; b = bottom; m = middle; l = left; r = right; bg = background)

Shutterstock: altanaka 8m; Chinnapong 19ml; Elena Barenbaum 19ml (bird); Emeryk III 8br; Hanet – all creatures, Jitlada Panwiset 4br; Lan Images 14bl; Macrovector 23t; Nanette Grebe 14br; Stig Alenas 19m.

3/20